THE SECRET TO GETTING LISTED AT THE TOP OF SEARCH ENGINES

BY

ALEXANDRA SAIEH

authorHOUSE®

AuthorHouse™
1663 Liberty Drive, Suite 200
Bloomington, IN 47403
www.authorhouse.com
Phone: 1-800-839-8640

First published by AuthorHouse 2/5/2008

ISBN: 978-1-4343-5453-2 (sc)

Library of Congress Control Number: 2008900236

Printed in the United States of America
Bloomington, Indiana
This book is printed on acid-free paper.

Notice of Liability

For my mother and father, Yolanda & Ted, who
continue to be an inspiration
in my life.

Acknowledgements:

I am grateful for everyone in my personal and professional network who offered me their knowledge, advice, and moral support.

To everyone at Author House who was involved in the editing, proofreading and layout of this book.

To my supportive and loving parents, siblings: Elizabeth, David, and Vanessa, as well as my friends. I would not have been able to write this book without your support. Elizabeth, thank you for assisting in the editing process as well.

To the clients of Stellar Image, you've allowed me to gain invaluable research through working on your online projects and have made it possible for me to share my knowledge with others.

Last, but certainly not least, thanks to you the readers.

CONTENTS

INTRODUCTION

And how this book differs from other SEO books

The Secret to Getting Listed at the Top of Search Engines will inform you about how search engines work and how to obtain higher search rankings. This book will put you in control of your own web site's search engine listing.

Whether or not you are a web designer, you will be able to positively transform your search engine rankings. The method to achieve top rankings in search engines will no longer be a mystery to you. I will show you, step by step, how to customize web pages to please the search engines and entice your customers at the same time.

The Secret to Getting Listed at the Top of Search Engines is based on the exact SEO tactics we use at my company, Stellar Image, LLC, to provide our clients with top rankings on search engines. Through my work and experience in SEO, I have determined the most effective tactics that will produce results. This book contains all these tactics in detail, in the order in which they should be employed. This alone will save you much time and money.

The way this book differs from other SEO books is that the extraneous technical details are excluded to allow the reader to grasp the most important information and act on it. It is also written in a concise and clear manner.

This book has been written with the online business owner in mind. I have outlined all the key points you need to include in optimizing your web site for top rankings. I have also included all of the web sites that I have found to be essential tools in the optimization process.

If you do not have a web site and are planning to design one or have one designed for you, this book will guide you in creating a user-friendly site that will achieve high rankings in search engines.

Alternatively, if you are a web designer and would like to offer SEO as an extra service, this book can outline the exact steps you need to take in order to get your clients' web sites highly ranked.

I have also made sure to keep the technical jargon to a minimum. It helps to know about coding, although it is not completely necessary. For information that includes coding, all you need to do is forward it to your web master, including the instructions in this book. Most of the code that needs to be added to your web site is minimal, yet essential.

Obtaining relevant inbound links and adding quality content on your web site is the majority of what needs to be added for your web site's success with the search engines.

I suggest you keep a notebook handy as you read this manual. You will need to make notes on what ways your web site needs to be changed and what code needs to be added, etc. Your notebook will also be necessary when you are writing extra content for your web site.

Introduction To SEO

I'd like to begin by providing a comprehensive definition for organic search engine optimization (SEO) and explaining how it differs from pay-per-click advertising. Organic SEO is the method of **developing and marketing** a web site so that it achieves higher ranking in search engine results pages, known as SERPs. Notice how I have highlighted the words developing and marketing. The actual development of your web site— such as proper code, content, and structure, plus the online marketing of your web site, such as link building— are the main tactics used in organic search engine optimization.

The development and marketing of your web site are further described by two categories: "on-page" and "off-page" optimization tactics. On-page tactics include any optimization tools that you implement in the actual pages of your web site and are considered development factors. Most on-page tactics include user-friendly page structure, keyword and meta tag inclusion, proper coding, and necessary content.

Off-page tactics include the optimization tools that have to do with the marketing and link building of your web site. Most off-page tactics involve choosing reputable web sites to exchange links with, placing links on reputable directories, and submitting articles and press releases.

The proper web site development and marketing is essentially the key to top search engine rankings. The search engines measure both the development and marketing of your web site when determining your rank; therefore, you must employ both to achieve top rankings.

The main feature of organic SEO is that you don't pay for each and every click, as in pay-per-click advertising. When your web site is optimized for organic search listings, it will be listed in the top SERPs shown on the left-hand side of the page. The listings displayed on the far right-hand column are those that require you to pay for each click and are essentially advertising through Google or other major search engines.

Reaching the top pages of organic listings will definitely take a while since your web site is one of more than a million web sites that are submitted to search engines on a regular basis. When you sign up for pay-per-click advertising, you can get listed that same day, although you will be paying for each and every click, whether it is a fraudulent click or not.

You can opt to run a pay-per-click campaign on one of the major search engines at the same time as you work on your organic SEO. It is your choice, although you need to be aware of the prevalence of fraudulent clicks at your expense.

Up to thirty percent of your pay-per-click charges can come from fraudulent clicks. Fraudulent clicks can come from many different areas, although the two most common sources are excessive clicks from competitors or individual web site owners/employees that display search engine ads to receive commissions.

Organic search engine optimization, on the other hand, is free to implement and a must-have for your web site. Organic SEO requires hard work and time, just like all great things, yet your web site will benefit from it greatly. More than 80 percent of all online traffic begins with a search on one of the search engines. Furthermore, since most web surfers do not look past the first one or two SERPs, you must constantly aim for top rankings.

CHAPTER 1

Search Engines and How They Work

Find out:

* How the search engines find and analyze web sites

* How search engines rank web sites

* What the Google sandbox is and how it can affect your web site

* The importance of your domain in search rankings

Chapter 1: Search Engines And How They Work

Where would the online community be without search engines? Search engines have become the sole source of organized information on the worldwide web. Visitors seeking information, products, or services go straight to their search engine of choice and expect to find exactly what they are looking for. Search engine companies know this and make it their priority to optimize their search results with the best results for each query.

Can you imagine what it would be like without the search engines? Visitors would need to memorize and bookmark the URLs of the web sites they found through printed sources or word of mouth.

Search engines exist to bring all types of information to the entire world. The search engines' main goal is to collect any and all pertinent information found in web sites, organize it, and make it easily accessible to millions of people.

Search engines now use a system of robots to scan ("crawl") entire web pages, including the meta tags and titles, because of the enormous volume of web sites in existence today. With the data collected from each web page, they score, index, and rank the web sites.

Search engines find out about a new web site through clicking on a link to it from another web site or when it is submitted to them for approval into their database.

The ranking system is performed with the use of algorithms, a set of rules that search engines use to evaluate a web site in determining its relevancy to a particular search.

Each major search engine uses its own methods and rules to produce search results, although most of the principles discussed in this book will always be necessary for web sites to have.

GOOGLE'S SANDBOX

Google is practically the most popular search engine on the web today. Most web site owners hire SEO companies to improve their listings in Google, since they know it is widely used. Yet it is important to know about the existence of "Google's sandbox," which applies to new web domains.

The Google sandbox method is used to place newly added web sites into a "sandbox" to evaluate them for an extensive period of time, during which the web sites receive poor ranking, although they are optimized properly.

When Google releases the web site from its sandbox, the web site can finally rank for popular keywords matching the data on its web site, as long as the web site is optimized properly. Generally speaking, it may take new web sites up to six to eight months to be able to achieve top rankings in Google results.

It may be frustrating, yet Google does this to analyze the web site during this time and make sure that it is a reputable site, with accurate and helpful information.

If you've owned a domain for a long period of time, you should not purchase a new one if the old one has a suitable name. The reason you should keep your older domain is because it will not be held in the sandbox for longer than a couple of months, even if you change the entire theme and design of the web site.

When a new domain is purchased, Google places it in the sandbox for about two to three months, regardless of how well it is written and designed.

There are some in the SEO industry that believe you should use a descriptive domain that matches your business or includes a keyword about your web site. I disagree with this notion and believe that the actual domain name has little impact on your rankings. The age of the domain name, however, is significant.

If you are interested in researching this topic further, you can perform searches for different topics and note the domain names of the top-ranking web sites. You will notice how many of the highly ranked web sites don't have a domain that matches the query.

In the following chapters, I will reveal all the tactics you need to use to achieve top rankings, gain more visibility, and increase visitors. You must follow each step in this book to achieve top rankings.

CHAPTER 2

Research Your Target Market

Find out:

* What your target market is

* What type of information you need to gather

* How you can use the information you collect

CHAPTER 2: RESEARCH YOUR TARGET MARKET

If you haven't already done so, your first step should be to identify your target market. In other words, determine what sector of the population your product or service is fit for. You need to define the exact details of this demographic in order to devise a way to get their attention when they are on your web site.

You will also use this information when you start choosing your keywords, which is discussed in detail in chapter four. Below are the details that you need to define about the target market for your product/service:

- Gender
- Age Group
- Geographic location
- Occupation
- Disposable income
- Likes and dislikes

The specifics of your target market will help you pinpoint the type of consumer that is most likely than others to make a purchase on your web site.

This will be very useful when choosing your keywords, since it will help you construct the decision process consumers go through when making a purchase. In addition, the characteristics of your target market will help you in providing content and incentives that address their needs.

You can also research what other types of web sites your target market visits for possible advertising opportunities. Without performing this type of research, you are basically guessing, which is pointless. You need to base your web site and SEO on solid research in order to reap the greatest benefits.

CHAPTER 2: ACTION STEPS TO TAKE

1. Define your target market in detail.

2. Find out what their likes and dislikes are, as well as their needs and lifestyles.

3. Search for web sites your target market visits and decide whether you should advertise on those web sites.

CHAPTER 3

Perform a Site Audit

Find out:

* What critical elements your
web site must have
for online success

* Why text links are better
than script links

* What critical errors to avoid

Chapter 3: Perform A Site Audit

Your second necessary step is to perform a complete site audit. The purpose of this site audit is to determine whether a change in certain design aspects, navigation, selling method, or a total redesign is necessary.

Whether you or one of your employees can perform this critical step in an objective manner is very important because you must make sure that you are starting off with a web site that is both user-friendly and search-engine-friendly. If the site audit cannot be performed objectively, it is necessary to hire an agency to perform the audit.

If you are just starting to build a web site, you can use these recommendations while you or your webmaster designs your site.

As the audit is being performed, it is also important to compare it to competitors' web sites. This will help in being more objective about your own web site and allow you to find ways in which you can outperform your competitors.

The following are very important rules to follow when performing a site audit:

1. The second visitors arrive at your web site, they must immediately be able to find out its purpose, or you may lose some visitors for not providing a solid theme.

2. Your visitors must be able to find other pages of your web site easily. (Search engine robots will also use your links to find your content.) Keep navigation clean and user-friendly. Also keep in mind that the search engines measure the amount of time visitors spend on your web site to judge the quality of your web site.

3. It's also best to have navigation links in two areas of your web pages. You could have a vertical navigation bar on the left-hand side of the page, with an additional set of links at the top or bottom of the page.

4. Place the majority of the links going to other pages of your site in text. Try to avoid placing links within images or flash, since search engine

robots cannot follow these links and will not be able to access the pages that the images link to. If you prefer to insert links in images/flash, make sure you place alternate text links elsewhere on the page.

5. Make sure that most of your web pages can be accessed within three clicks or less from the home page. This will make it easier for the search engines to find your pages.

6. Use proper grammar and correct spelling. Spelling your keywords and content correctly is essential. You cannot rank well for keywords if you misspell them. Also, your web site will maintain its credibility by using correct grammar and spelling.

7. Avoid the use of frames and limit the use of dynamic web pages. Dynamic pages are those that contain information from an outside database file and end with a question mark or other symbol. It is difficult and sometimes impossible for search engine robots to access information in this type of programming. Your index page (home page) should always end with an .html or .htm.

8. Use small amounts of JavaScript and provide an additional set of text links if you use JavaScript for your main navigation menu.

9. Avoid using too many graphics/large graphics, extensive animation, or flash. If your web site contains most animation/flash in the header or a few pages, it is okay if the rest of your web site contains plenty of text. The main reason for minimizing the use of animation/flash is that search engines cannot read text in flash or graphics.

10. Do not use bright colors such as hot pink or canary yellow for your background or in large areas of your web site. Your goal is to keep visitors on your web site for an extensive period of time, and bright colors are hard on the eyes.

11. Make sure you or your web designer programs your web site with html code that contains few errors and avoids broken tags and links. You can validate your code with the W3C markup validator at: http://validator.w3.org.

   It is okay to have up to fifty errors per page or so as long as your links work and you provide the following statement at the top of your html pages, announcing that your page is "transitional":

<!DOCTYPE HTML PUBLIC "-//W3C//DTD HTML 4.01 Transitional//EN">.

12. Make sure that your web site is not entirely coded in PHP, because search engines may have difficulty accessing all your web pages. The same is true for any web pages that can only be accessed by a member login.

13. If a web page has been deleted, make sure you offer a redirect to a different page or create a unique 404 error page to provide a link to visitors that takes them back to your home page.

14. Do not include any outbound links on your home page. You don't want visitors to leave your site prematurely. If you prefer to have outbound links on your web site, place the code "target=_blank" into the link so that it will open up in a new window and your web site will remain in the background (or in another tab in Internet Explorer 7 (IE 7)) so the visitor can go back to it, e.g.:

```
<a href="www.yahoo.com" target="_blank"
>Yahoo</a>
```

15. Avoid the use of welcome pages: entry pages that are provided as an introduction to the entire web site, containing a link to access the web site. Some search engine robots may stop at this welcome page, ignore the link to the rest of the site, and leave without ever scanning the important part of the web site.

16. Do not use small and hard-to-read text. Your visitors will find it annoying and search engines will find it deceiving.

17. The more quality content you provide, the more search engines and visitors will recognize your site as an informative and useful one.

    o The content must be directly related to your product and/or service and the keywords you choose to optimize the page.

    o You will receive the benefit of viral marketing, which is essentially word of mouth and social bookmarking on sites like www.digg.com.

o This is a great way to build credibility and trust, which are necessary if you want to sell on the Internet.

My article, *Signs You May Need a New Web Design*, is also helpful to read, and you can find it here:

www.stellarimagedesign.com/website-redesign.html.

CHAPTER 3: ACTION STEPS TO TAKE

1. Analyze your web site to make sure it is user-friendly and search-engine-friendly.
   a. Use simple navigation.
   b. Don't use too many graphics.
   c. Minimize the use of animation and/or flash.
   d. Use proper grammar and correct spelling.
   e. Validate your code and check for errors.

2. Analyze your competitors' web sites.
   a. Check to see how they address their customers.
   b. Study how much content your competitors provide.

CHAPTER 4

Keyword Usage and Meta Tags

Find out:

* How to come up with the best keywords

* Why the right keywords are extremely important

* Where the keywords need to be inserted

* How to measure keyword density

Chapter 4: Keyword Usage And Meta Tags

Keyword usage is essentially the keywords you list in your code that accurately describe the content of your web site. Keyword analysis is the method of researching the proper keywords you would like your web site to rank highly for. Choosing the right keywords requires a good amount of research and provides the foundation for your entire web site optimization.

The keywords you choose must be directly related to your business and the products and/or services you offer. The reason you need to research your keywords is because some will be more profitable than others, while some keywords will just be extremely competitive and difficult to optimize for.

Keywords can be comprised of one word or a phrase. These keywords are inserted in your web site's code, in special tags known as meta tags, which I will discuss in detail a bit later. Keywords provide the foundation for your web site because your overall content needs to include them and your entire web site must be focused on these keywords. They will be inserted in specific areas of your web site and in outbound and inbound links.

To determine the validity of your web site, most search engines will actually measure how many times your keywords appear in your web site's content. This is known as keyword density and is basically the ratio of keywords to total words on a page. You always want to strive for 1–2 percent density, which means that out of one hundred words of text on your web page (including links), your keyword appears one to two times.

It may sound simple, yet it's not so simple when keeping in mind that the text needs to sound interesting to your visitors as well. After all, your ultimate goal is to entice your visitors to make a purchase.

The following are several web sites that will measure the keyword density of your content:

http://www.live-keyword-analysis.com

http://www.webjectives.com/keyword.htm

Through trial and error, I have found that if you achieve the keyword density of 1–2 percent for about three or four of your keywords, this should be plenty. If you flood your content by including more than three or four keywords that are mentioned several times, the search engines may consider this spam and will penalize your web site.

To avoid getting banned from the search engines, I recommend staying within the 1–2 percent keyword density range for up to three keywords. I also suggest including an average of four hundred words of text per web page that you want to optimize.

Having said this, I do not want you to think you need to provide a large amount of pages with the keyword density of 1–2 percent. You should aim for at least three to five pages with this keyword density, along with some other content-filled pages to support these five pages. This amount will differ according to how many pages your competition has.

If your competing web sites have twenty or more content-filled pages, you should provide the same amount and possibly more if you want to outrank your competitors.

In researching a variety of keywords, I have found that phrases with two to five words are the most profitable. They are also the type of descriptions people search for when they are ready to purchase.

I highly advise you to choose keywords that are attainable. For example, let's say an online merchant owns a twenty-page web site that sells jewelry and this person has optimized it in every way possible, following all known search engine rules. There is practically no chance at all that the web site can rank higher than a web site that has one hundred plus pages, more incoming links/visitors, and ranks at the top of the list for a common and highly competitive keyword such as "jewelry."

The reason for this is that a web site must be comparable, in each and every aspect, to the competing site it is to replace in the SERPs, although I am not suggesting that you copy your competitor's web site and/or content.

To be an equal match, your web site must contain all the positive attributes that allow the competing web site to rank highly, such as amount of pages, quality content, substantial quality links/traffic, clean code, etc. This successful competitor also took quite a while to get where it is, most likely a year or more.

Smaller to medium businesses must realize that the keywords they use do not have to be the most competitive. There is just too much competition out there, and these highly competitive keywords are usually not as profitable anyway.

The more profitable keywords tend to be more specific keyword phrases, usually between two to five words, such as "sterling silver earrings on sale," for example. These long tail phrases are much less competitive and convert to sales pretty well, given you spend time extensively researching keywords. I recommend the following professional service for providing one of the best keyword research tools:

www.keyworddiscovery.com.

You will be able to search for the least competitive and most popular keywords for a given topic. These are the types of keywords you want to choose for your web site. Another web site you will find very useful is:

www.seologs.com/keyword-difficulty.html.

At this web site, you can determine what keywords are most competitive and/or difficult to rank highly for. This will save you much time when deciding what keywords to use. When using the tool on this web site, choose the keywords that have a keyword difficulty measure somewhere in the middle or lower end of the bar. Avoid the keywords that have a high difficulty measure.

You should also take a peak at the keywords your top competitors are using for guidance. You can do this by viewing their web site's source code to look for their meta tags, which are located at the top of the source page. You can view the source page by clicking on file, then view, and then source in the Internet Explorer menu (view source in Firefox). The exact html code of the web page will then be displayed in a separate text file. The meta keywords will be written exactly like the example below:

<meta name="keywords" content="**dedicated hosting, web design, web templates, add music to web site**">

I have highlighted the keywords in bold. This is what you need to analyze. If your competitor is at the top of the SERPs for a keyword you desire, you should use similar, if not identical, keywords. Just make sure you don't violate any copyrights or trademarks by copying any words or phrases they have protected.

You should also be aware that some web sites block their source code so you will not be able to see it.

Most words or phrases commonly used in the English language are safe to use, such as web design, web hosting, inexpensive web design, etc. Also keep in mind that you need to be able to provide plenty of content to insert these keywords into.

I also recommend limiting the amount of keywords for your web site to ten per page. If you go over ten keywords, then it will be very difficult to add content on one page to cover all these keywords. If you stick to less than ten important keywords, and strive for the 1–2 percent keyword density for only three of them, they will not be diluted with other less significant keywords. Your web site will then be tightly focused on your important topics so that search engines will not have a hard time determining what your web site is about.

If you are targeting a specific area, such as the city you are based in, you can include the city and state in your keywords. This will help you rank higher when a searcher includes the city and state, which is often the case when they are searching for a local business. You should also include your physical address, including the city and state, on your contact page and your home page or "about us" page.

Once you have your keyword list, you will use it to compose the meta tags and html tags that define your site's title and description, and inform the search engines about your web site's main topic.

Most search engines will not even index your web site if it does not contain meta tags. I have included the meta tags we use for one of the web pages on www. stellarimagedesign.com below. The meta tags are inserted between the "HEAD" tags of each page. Insert them in each and every page of your web site and just replace our title, keywords, and description with yours. Follow the recommendations listed just below the code as well.

<head>

<meta http-equiv="Content-Type" content="text/html; charset=ISO-8859-1">

<meta name="robots" content="index,follow" />

<meta name="Googlebot" content="index,follow" />

<META NAME="Keywords" CONTENT="austin SEO, search engine optimization, austin, tx, search engine ranking, search engine placement, search engine marketing, search engine submission, SEO training">

<META NAME="Description" CONTENT="Austin SEO: Austin, TX Search Engine Optimization, SEO services with proven results. Free SEO guidelines and articles. SEO training and services offered.">

<title>Austin SEO: Search Engine Optimization for Small to Medium Online Businesses - SEO Training on Ranking, Optimization and Content</title>

<meta name="ROBOTS" content="all">

</head>

Title Tag: The title tag begins with <TITLE> and ends with </TITLE>. Make a short and distinctive title for each web page. It should be between ten and fifty characters and should include your most important keywords. Every main word of the title should begin with a capital letter. You should refrain from using extraneous words, such as welcome to our web site, etc. This way, the title will be primarily focused on your keywords. I believe the title tag to be the most important tag of all.

Keyword Tag: The keyword tag begins with <meta name="keywords" content= " and ends with ">. The keywords tag is where you insert the keywords that you researched for your web site as indicated earlier in this chapter. It should include no more than 50-150 characters.

Description Tag: The description tag begins with <meta name="description" content=" and ends with ">. Your description should consist of a meaningful sentence about your business and should include no more than 10 keywords and 150–200 characters. The description should contain your most important keywords. Stay away from excessive use of keywords, exaggeration, unrelated comments, and exclamation marks.

All the information contained in these meta tags is not case-sensitive, although I recommend using all lowercase letters, except for the initial letter of each word in the title. You can also capitalize certain words in the description, which will usually be used for the description in your search engine listing.

It is important to choose different keywords, titles, and descriptions for different web pages if the pages cover different topics. For instance, if your web site's main purpose is to promote the shoes and clothing your company sells, you would optimize the page displaying the shoes with keywords and content about shoes. On the separate page that displays the clothing, you would optimize the page with keywords and content about clothes.

You do not need to include your keywords in the domain name. As I mentioned in chapter one, your domain has little impact on your rankings. Therefore, if you are searching for a domain name for your web site, choose one that would be easy for your customers to remember so that they can easily refer you to their friends and family. After all, word-of-mouth advertising is very powerful. You can search for hundreds of domains on: www.stellarimagedesign.com/webhosting.html at the bottom of the page.

The age of the domain name, on the other hand, is very important. The older a domain is, the more it is trusted by the search engines.

A note about keyword density: As mentioned previously, include the majority of your keywords in the actual text of your web site and preferably in the first half of your page.

A note about content writing: Write content specific to your target market and offer easy ordering methods. Appeal to your customers and their preferences and offer useful material. You may have seen the phrase "content is king" before, and I am emphasizing it once again.

Quality content is one of the most important factors that search engines consider in ranking your web site. The importance of your web site is primarily determined by the freshness, uniqueness, and quantity of its content.

Also keep the following in mind: if your content is important to your visitors, it will be important to search engines.

CHAPTER 4: ACTION STEPS TO TAKE

1. Research the proper keywords to use for your web site.

    a. Remember that your keywords need to match the theme and purpose of your web site.

    b. You will need to provide plenty of content on your web pages to include these keywords in.

2. Use the online tools mentioned in this chapter to determine the demand and competition for each keyword you intend to use.

    a. Only use the keywords that have low to medium competition and a relatively high demand.

3. Check which keywords your competitors are using.

4. Include the keywords in your content while staying within a keyword density of 1–2 percent.

5. Compose your meta tags.

CHAPTER 5

The Need for Content Writing

Find out:

* What and how much content
is recommended for
online success

* The important issues to
consider when writing content

* What page of your web site is
most important

* What link bait is and how it
can help your web site

Chapter 5: The Need For Content Writing

The readable text throughout your web site is known as content. Content is one of the most important elements of a web site that influences its overall search rankings. The two most important points to keep in mind when you are writing content for your web site are:

- The content must be original and cannot be a duplicate of any other web page. Duplicate content is damaging to your search rankings.
- The majority of the content must match or be similar to the topic of your web site, keywords you choose, and products you sell and/or services you provide.

As discussed in the previous chapter, your keywords must be included in the majority of the content, while keeping the keyword density at 1–2 percent. It's safe to say that you can never have too much content. Search engines love content, and they prefer it to be updated on a regular basis.

If you are too busy to write extensive amounts of content on a regular basis, you can search for content copy writers on the Internet that specialize in content that is search-engine-friendly.

Adding new, focused content is a good SEO tactic to use for maintaining top search rankings. Just remember to keep web pages less than eight hundred words long and to use correct spelling and grammar.

Although original content is always most important, you can also include articles from other sources, as long as you follow the writer's/publisher's rules and provide proper credits. These articles do help, yet not nearly as much as original content.

THE TRUST FACTOR

Trust is one of the most important factors when referring to visitors and search engines. You must provide helpful, useful information that ties into your web site theme in order to gain the respect and trust of your visitors and search engines. Visitors will not order from you and search engines will not rank you highly if your web site is not professional and user-friendly.

I have included some helpful suggestions for any type of web site:

- Keep your web site clean and easy to navigate through. You want to make it easy for the search engine robots to read all of the information on your web site, and you surely want your visitors to find their way through the ordering process as easily as possible.

- Your web site should have few spelling mistakes and broken links. Both displease readers by appearing unprofessional, and broken links have a negative impact on your search rankings. As mentioned earlier, if your keywords are misspelled, you will not be able to rank highly for them.

- Provide plenty of testimonials from satisfied customers. This will enhance the trust factor and serve as additional content as well.

- Make sure you provide a contact name, address, e-mail, and phone number. Many web visitors prefer to contact an actual person before ordering. Including your address will allow your web site to be listed when people search for the specific products or services in your area.

LINK BAIT

The term link bait refers to online content that attracts other web site owners to link to it because of its unique value. Content that offers unique and, in some way, remarkable information attracts others to link to it. If you can write content that is very helpful and innovative, you will receive many links from happy readers, which will greatly improve your search rankings.

KEYWORDS INCLUDED IN ANCHOR TEXT

Including your keywords in anchor text refers to the inclusion of your keywords in a link to another page on your web site. Again, you should try to stay within the 1–2 percent keyword density recommendation so your content won't be considered spam. Search engines regard anchor text as highly important, and you should try to include it with your keywords in the web pages you want optimized.

THE HOME PAGE IS NUMBER ONE

The most important web page you need to optimize for the search engines is your home page. Most often than not, the search engines will consider it as your landing page. Therefore, you must spend the most time optimizing the home page — more than any other page on your site. Most importantly, a large amount of your backlinks should direct visitors to your home page. You should also provide a sufficient amount of optimized content on the home page as well.

SIMPLE NAVIGATION STRUCTURE

You definitely want to make sure that most of your web pages are accessible through the home page. If your web site has more than thirty pages, you could have some pages accessible within two to three links from your home page.

USE HEADINGS AND SUBHEADINGS

The use of headings and subheadings will help the search engine robots organize your information by importance. Always use the header tags to identify headings and subheadings, for example:

<H1>Search Engine Optimization</H1>

This also helps visitors read your content, since it's more difficult to read from a computer screen than from print. In addition, most readers do not read all of the content on a web page so headings make it easier for visitors to find what they are looking for.

ADD MINIMAL COPY WHERE NEEDED

You want to keep certain web pages of your web site free of too much copy if the page's purpose requires it. You certainly don't have to have a large amount of content on every single page of your web site; just enough content throughout your web site. For example, you don't need to add several paragraphs to the web page that contains the order information. However, I do recommend providing a minimum of three to five web pages containing four hundred words of content.

CHAPTER 5: ACTION STEPS TO TAKE

1. Write interesting, original content for your web site that includes your keywords.

   a. Make sure that the content is useful and helpful to visitors.

2. Include your keywords in most of the anchor text.

3. Spend the most time optimizing your home page.

4. Use headings and subheadings while including them in the header tags.

5. Provide testimonials from satisfied customers.

6. Provide adequate contact information.

CHAPTER 6

Search Submission and PR/Article Submission

Find out:

* Where you need to submit your web site to the search engines

* When and how often you should submit your web site

* What submission sites to steer clear from

* How to submit press releases and articles about your web site

Chapter 6: Search Submission And Pr/article Submission

Now that your web site has been optimized, it is time to submit it to the major search engines. You should submit your web site at this time because you need to have your web site optimized to be listed well. You can submit your site before you build your entire link popularity and content, because the search engines can take up to six months to evaluate and index your site.

In my experience, it is more important to work on your keywords, meta tags, and content prior to submittal. You do not need to build up your complete link popularity prior to submittal. You can work on your link popularity soon after you submit to the search engines, while you are waiting to be indexed.

The reason for this is that the search engines will have listed your web site in their large database of web sites to evaluate but will not actually evaluate the entire web site and backlinks until about a month after that. In the next chapter, I will show you how to submit your web site to reputable directories and build links in other ways.

I have listed the major search engines and the URLs to go to so that you can submit your site:

- Google: http://www.google.com/addurl/ ?continue=/addurl
- Yahoo: http://search.yahoo.com/info/submit. html
- MSN: http://beta.search.msn.co.uk/docs/ submit.aspx?FORM=WSUT
- ISEDN: http://www.isedn.org

You do not have to submit to other, less popular search engines, because the above four major search engines provide the search results for the smaller search engines as follows:

- Google provides its direct organic search results and paid listings to AOL Search, Ask. com, and Netscape Search. In turn, Ask.com then provides direct organic search results to Lycos and Iwon Search.

- Yahoo provides its direct organic search results and paid listings to Alltheweb and Altavista.

You may have seen some web sites offering to submit your web site to over ten thousand search engines, when in fact most of these so-called search engines are merely FFA (free for all) directories that are not considered reputable to the search engines. You should avoid submitting your web site to these sites.

As you submit your web site, just enter the entire URL of your web site: http://www.yourwebsite.com. You do not need to submit all of the other pages of your web site to the search engines, since they will visit those pages from the links on your home page. Once again, make sure that all of your web pages can be accessed from your home page or within one to two links from the home page.

The search engines will not list your web site right away. It can take anywhere from three to six months to have your site listed in the search engines, depending on the age of your web site, actual number of pages of quality content your web site contains, link popularity, and other factors.

Search engines exist to provide relevant information to visitors and are constantly refining their algorithms to make sure that their visitors' needs are met. Each search engine has different algorithms that it uses to determine a web site's relevance for a certain search query and weighs the various SEO factors differently. For instance, you may end up being listed higher in Ask.com than in Google. The search engines do not reveal all of their algorithms to the public, so it is very important that you monitor your listings, keywords, and competition on a constant basis.

You may have already heard of Google's page ranking method. PageRank (PR) is a number assigned to each web site on the Internet that ranges between zero and ten. Google's page rank affects the Google rank of a web site on the SERPs and is primarily determined by how many reputable backlinks the web site has.

In addition, most highly ranked web sites on the Internet are given a page rank of at least four by Google. Most large, high-traffic web sites with more than fifty pages receive a higher page rank as well. The way you can analyze page ranks is by downloading the Google toolbar for Internet Explorer at: http://toolbar.google. com/T4/index_pack.html.

For those of you who use Firefox, the Google toolbar already comes with it. You can spot Google's PageRank close to the middle of the toolbar, displayed as a small bar. You can actually see the PR number for the given web site that you are currently on by simply placing your cursor over the bar.

The PR number displayed is generally a good estimate, since it is not updated on a timely basis. It is my understanding that Google developed the page ranking system to show how "important" each web site is.

If you do not want to download the Google toolbar, another way to check your web site's PageRank, and that of any other web site, is by going to: http://www. digpagerank.com and typing in the URL of the web site.

Once you have submitted your site to the search engines, you will not need to resubmit it until you make any major changes to the content or navigation. Anytime you make these changes, you can resubmit to the major search engines I mentioned above. You should also update your site map with the new pages.

I recommend that you limit your submissions to every four to eight weeks. The new web pages and/or content that you add will also take a while to be indexed. After visiting your new content, the search engines go through a method of scanning the content to evaluate it and make sure it does not violate any rules.

The search engines will then index your new pages, usually within twelve weeks or so. If your web site has a page rank of four or above and has been indexed by the search engine for several months prior to the resubmission, your new content can be indexed within one to two weeks, as I have witnessed with our web site, www.stellarimagedesign.com.

SUBMIT PRESS RELEASES AND ARTICLES

One of the best ways to generate buzz and interest about your web site is to write articles and press releases. If you'd like to see examples of articles you can submit, you can read one of my articles at:

www.stellarimagedesign.com/websitetips.html.

Notice how our articles are all focused on the topic of web design and search engine optimization. When you submit your articles, make sure you write them yourself and stay focused on your product and/or service. You can write about a closely related topic as well, as long as it will lure readers to your web site.

TIPS ON WRITING PRESS RELEASES

When you write press releases about your web site, they need to read like a news story. As such, you cannot include any type of promotional messages or jargon. Doing so may prevent your press release from being accepted or distributed.

Keep press releases short and sweet. You want your audience to capture the purpose of your release without being too wordy. You should also stay away from writing long paragraphs or stretching the truth. Most well-written press releases are one page long and present the facts in a clear, concise manner.

The press releases you write should definitely keep the reader interested. You should try to provide as much creativity as possible while being newsworthy.

I suggest you submit one to two articles or press releases per month for the first six to eight months. After that you can submit an article or press release every few months or so. For press release examples, you can refer to the following web sites, which also provide instructions:

http://www.publicityinsider.com/release.asp

http://www.prwebdirect.com/pressreleasetips.php

WHERE TO SUBMIT

You can submit your articles to these top submission web sites and search for others to submit to in Google:

http://ezinearticles.com — This web site is for providers of e-zines and newsletters that search for new and interesting content to provide their readers.

http://www.articlepr.com — This web site has an entire list of article directories to submit to.

You can submit your press releases to any of these top submission web sites and search for others to submit to in Google:

http://www.newswiretoday.com/index.php

http://www.przoom.com

http://www.pressexposure.com

CHAPTER 6: ACTION STEPS TO TAKE

1. Submit your web site to the major search engines as discussed in this chapter.

2. Resubmit your web site to the search engines each time you make major changes/additions to the web site.

3. Submit press releases and articles to the submission web sites mentioned in this chapter.
   a. Try to submit at least one article or press release per month for the first six to eight months.

CHAPTER 7

Keep a Constant Watch on Your Competition and Market

Find out:

* What you need to research about your competition and market

* What tools can help you in the research process

* What characteristics of a web site make it difficult to outrank

Chapter 7: Keep A Constant Watch On Your Competition And Market

Now that you know what keywords you want to use, the next thing you must do is research your competition. What I mean by this is to identify only your competition that currently has the top rankings (SERPs) for the keywords that you desire and then study their web site to the letter.

Every industry will differ in certain ways, but as a general rule, you must analyze your competitors very closely since you must replace their listing with yours. The bottom line is this: you have to outperform your competitors' optimization tactics in order to rank above them in the SERPs. I know it sounds fierce, but competition is what search engine optimization is all about!

In a nutshell, the following factors are what you need to research about your competitors:

- Research their meta tags and keywords. As mentioned in chapter three, you can do this by clicking on view in the Internet Explorer menu (view source in Firefox) and then clicking on source. This shows you the exact html code of the web page.

- Literally count how many pages and text the competing web site has and compare it to your web site. Microsoft Word has a built-in word count application you can find under the tools tab. Just copy and paste the text on your competitor's web site and use the word-count tool. If your web site does not come close to the amount of pages and content the other web site has, it will be difficult to rank above it in the search engines.

- You can conduct a backlink report on your competitors' web sites to check how many web sites link to them. That way you can add as many links as they have to be able to outrank them. The best method for checking backlinks is provided by Yahoo at https://siteexplorer.search.yahoo.com.

You will need to log in with a yahoo account, which is free. Once logged in, you will see a search box at the top. Type in the URL of the web site you would like to analyze and hit enter. Toward the top of the next page, you will see the results and a link that says: Inlinks (298). The number in parentheses will be different with every web site. This is the number of backlinks the web site has, and you just need to click on this link to see the detailed list of each web site that links to the one you are researching.

You can also check the backlinks of any web site by going to Google and entering the following phrase in the search bar: link: www.yourwebsite.com. Yet keep in mind that Google discloses far less actual backlinks than Yahoo. The Yahoo tool is a more accurate measure.

It's also a good idea to perform a thorough online market analysis. To perform an effective online market analysis, you should study forums and blogs that focus on your product and/or service category, in addition to conventional marketing research methods.

This will allow you to read about what customers are saying about your type of product, service, and even competitors. This information can be very helpful in determining the needs and wants of your online target market.

You can also study the web sites of indirect competitors that are located in other areas of the U.S., as well as in your direct market. The reason for doing this is so that you can follow the current online trend in your industry and make adjustments to offer a top-of-the-line web site for your target market.

Please be aware that some of your competitors will be extremely difficult to outrank because of their popularity, traffic, and other factors.

CHAPTER 7: ACTION STEPS TO TAKE

1. Analyze your competitors' meta tags and keywords.

2. Count how many pages and text the competing web sites have.

3. Conduct a backlink report on your competitors' web sites.

4. Study forums and blogs that focus on your product and/or service category.

5. Make adjustments to your web site after studying the material you gather from other web sites.

CHAPTER 8

Other Necessary Files

Find out:

* What type of files will help
search engines access
the information on
your web site

* How to construct the files
to improve your web site
ranking

* Which folders these files
should be placed in

Chapter 8: Other Necessary Files

This chapter shows you how to add code that is essential to helping search engine robots figure out how to read through the information on your web site.

ALT TAGS

Alt tags are attributes included in your image link to describe what the graphic is about. Since search engine robots cannot see images, you need to provide a quick definition for each graphic on your site. The code will look like this (with your keywords contained inside the quotation marks): alt="dedicated web hosting, unlimited emails." You can insert it right before the image tag ends like this: <img src="images/hosting.jpg" alt="dedicated web hosting, unlimited emails">.

ROBOT TEXT DOC

The robot text document is a simple text file of instructional code that alerts the search engine robots what to do with the information found on your web site. It also serves the purpose of allowing you to block unimportant files or any content that may be difficult for robots to crawl. I have listed the exact details you need to include in this text document below:

User-agent:*

Disallow: /otherfiles

Disallow: /cgi-bin

The meaning of the above code is:

User-agent:*— This top line of code just means that the instructions apply to all the search engines. If you wish to specifically address a certain search engine, just type the name of the search engine robot, e.g. googlebot for google:

User-agent: googlebot

Each search engine has its own robot that you can become familiar with. You can view the names in your web log files or robot visitor stats.

This means that when you type the above line before the ones below, you are telling Google's robot, googlebot, to follow the instructions below:

Disallow: /otherfiles

Disallow: /cgi-bin

What the two lines mean above is that you are instructing the designated search engine robots to ignore whatever is in the folders named "otherfiles" and "cgi-bin."

Even if you'd like the robots to scan your entire web site, you still need to include the disallow line. Just leave it blank like this:

Disallow:

Now all you need to do is to name and save the file as text like this: robots.txt. Then upload it to your web site's root directory, where your index.html file is placed. The search engines should be able to access it at: http://www.yourwebsite.com/robots.txt.

SITE MAP

I also highly recommend including a site map for your web site that can be accessed in your web site's main directory, just like the robots file: http://www.yourwebsite.com/sitemap.html. The site map should contain each page of your web site with an optional description, although descriptions must be kept relatively short. The site map serves as a road map to guide search engine robots through your web site. It is also useful to your visitors as well. You can generate an .xml version instead if you are familiar with XML by using the free tool provided at www.xml-sitemaps.com. A good sitemaps how-to web site is www.sitemaps.org.

CHAPTER 8: ACTION STEPS TO TAKE

1. Make sure each graphic contains a descriptive alt tag, e.g.:
   <img src="images/pic.jpg" alt="web design">

2. Compose your robot text file as outlined in this chapter, and upload it to your web site's root directory. If you basically want all search engines to scan your entire web site, your text file will look like this:
   User-agent:*
   Disallow:

3. Compose your site map and upload it to your web site's root directory.

CHAPTER 9

Mind Your Link Popularity

Find out:

* How you can increase your web site's link popularity

*The importance of directory listings

* What tools will help you throughout the link building process

Chapter 9: Mind Your Link Popularity

Link popularity is defined by the number of web sites that have direct links to your site, commonly referred to as backlinks. The system of building link popularity is known as link building. This is also a very important step because search engines consider your site more important when other quality web sites link to it. Each inbound link counts as a "vote" for your web site. The more votes your web site has, the higher ranking it will receive, provided that you follow the other suggestions in this book.

In fact, most of the major search engines view link popularity as one of the most important factors in determining rankings. Now these web sites do need to be directly related to your general topic or they won't count very much. Links from .org or .edu web sites are deemed very highly, as well as web sites that are directly related to your products or services.

Do yourself a favor and DO NOT purchase links on other web sites. The reason is that never before has this one step been so frowned upon until now. For reasons that are unknown, Google is outwardly asking web visitors to report links that they believe to have been paid for so that they can be discounted. These do not include paid directories or paid search engine listings.

The best way to obtain high quality links is to obtain links from other highly ranked web sites and to submit your site to quality directories. You'd be surprised how many free quality directories there are available. When requesting links or submitting to directories, make sure that the backlink to your web site contains at least two of your chosen keywords inside the anchor text to improve your rankings.

All directories have categories and subcategories. It is important to choose an appropriate category to list your web site under and provide a good title/description, because an actual human will decide whether or not to accept your submission.

As mentioned earlier, not only are many links important, but most of these links should also come from reputable sites and sites that are generally related to your topic. To make sure the web site is reputable, you could check their Google PR (page rank) to make sure it is at least a three. General business directories are also beneficial to use if you are targeting businesses, and home directories are good to use if you are targeting home owners, for example. You can also submit your web site to the free yellow pages directories.

I have listed some free/inexpensive, reputable directories to get you started:

www.eplanit.biz

www.aboutd.com

www.resourcelinks.net

www.worlddirectory.com

www.btobonlinedirectory.com

www.alistdirectory.com

www.alistsites.com

www.directoryvault.com

www.freewebsitedirectory.com

www.info-listings.com

www.turnpike.net

You can also perform a Google search for quality directories. You could search for "web directories," for example, and submit your site to the directories with page ranks of three or more. It is also important to add your web site to Google's and Yahoo's local search. To sign up, go to the following sites:

Google: www.google.com/local/add

Yahoo: http://local.yahoo.com

Another great way to find reputable directories is to perform a search for your industry directories, e.g. gourmet food directories. Then choose the top directories, listed on the first two pages of the search results, to submit to.

You should not have to pay much, if at all, for a directory listing or provide a reciprocal link. Submit to the directories that are free and do not require a reciprocal link. If a directory requires a small fee, it could be worth getting listed in if it is highly reputable and is directly related to your web site.

If you sell products on your web site, you should also submit your web site to the popular shopping directories, such as:

http://shopping.yahoo.com

http://www.google.com/products

You can also search for quality shopping directories on Google.

Keep in mind that your directory listing will need to be approved by the directory and this can take up to one to two months. Also when checking your backlinks, note that the backlink report will not include a directory listing until it has been approved. Do not get discouraged when you see less than ten backlinks pointing to your web site after a few weeks of submitting to more than one hundred directories. Link building takes time.

If you are looking to improve your rankings in Google alone, you need to obtain more backlinks from web sites that have the same or similar keywords as your web site.

You will need to monitor your backlinks at least once every three months to make sure you maintain them at this web site:

https://siteexplorer.search.yahoo.com.

Follow the instructions I provided in chapter seven. You should also continue to obtain quality links on a regular basis.

CHAPTER 9: ACTION STEPS TO TAKE

1. Build your link popularity by submitting your web site to reputable directories and related web sites.

2. Submit your web site to Google's and Yahoo's local search directories.

3. Compare the number of backlinks your site has with that of your competition.

4. If you wish to surpass a certain competitor's listing, add more backlinks to your web site in order to exceed the competitor's number of backlinks.

5. Monitor your backlinks every three months.

6. Obtain quality links on a regular basis.

CHAPTER 10

Search Engines of the Future

Find out:

* What the online community expects from search engines in the future

* How you can prepare your web site for future search engine changes

Chapter 10: Search Engines Of The Future

The search engines are, by no means, perfect. As of now, search studies reveal that searchers often need to search more than once to find what they are looking for. In a recent press release, Google announced that it has been making changes to its algorithms, hardware, and software to address this issue. It is probable that other search engines will follow in Google's footsteps to remain competitive.

In the near future, the online community expects the major search engines to deliver more relevant results. In other words, search engines will be able to provide more specific information for improved accuracy. This will speed up the searching process and enhance user experience. On the other hand, web owners will need to add a few more tactics to their organic SEO efforts.

To provide more specific information, search engines will be switching to a universal search method, which is defined by offering results consisting of all types of media, in addition to content found in web pages.

Google has started taking the first steps by adding an image search, news search, blog search, and video search. These search categories have their own unique and separate databases of information. Yet in the future, the major search engines will integrate all of the video, image, blog, news, and web page data to produce more complete search results.

What this translates to is a need for web owners to provide adequate information in all the following areas: news articles/press releases, videos, images, and blogs. We don't know when the universal search method will be complete, yet Google reports that it will develop the method in stages. Therefore, it is a good idea to start providing this information as early as you can.

Providing images on your web site with detailed alt tags, as described in chapter eight, is relatively easy. You probably have images on your web site already. You were also given information on how to submit articles and press releases in chapter six. As for videos, you can hire someone to produce them for you, although it is not an immediate thing that you need to implement.

One thing you should definitely consider doing is creating a blog or forum and posting articles and comments to it on a regular basis. Blogs and forums not only serve as additional content on your site but also as an informational community for your visitors. They can sign up to be able to post comments and/or additional information. This in turn creates interest and word-of-mouth advertising.

LAST-MINUTE MUST-DO

Once you have created a blog, image, video, or article, you can submit it and any other important content about your web site, such as product details and job postings, to Google Base: http://base.google.com/base.

Don't forget to do this, because along with following the rest of the guidelines in this book, performing this step should greatly improve your rankings.

CHAPTER 10: ACTION STEPS TO TAKE

1. In the near future, start to provide a blog or forum on your web site, as long as you have the time to do it.

2. Remember to submit articles and press releases on a regular basis.

3. Submit any articles, press releases, products and/or services to Google Base.

4. Incorporate videos on your web site in the future if you have time and money to do so.

CHAPTER 11

Keep Your Top Rankings

Find out:

* What design elements will lower search engine listings

* What tactics you need to perform to maintain top search engine listings

Chapter 11: Keep Your Top Rankings

BY AVOIDING THESE TACTICS:

- Don't drastically change the topic of your home page or any other page of your web site that has been highly ranked, unless you are planning to change businesses. The reason for this is that some search engines, particularly Google, may assume that your domain has been purchased by a different company or owner, and this may result in much lower rankings, or it may take several months to rank higher for keywords.

- NEVER try to trick the search engines by using unethical methods, known as black hat SEO. This can lead to your site being banned from their search results and/or index. Below are some tactics used to trick the search engines, which you must avoid:

o Keyword stuffing is basically inserting an exaggerated amount of keywords in the text of your web site.

o Invisible text is the practice of inserting a large amount of keywords in white text on a white background, whether the keywords are related to the web site content or not.

o Doorway pages are html pages that are optimized with a large amount of keywords and are designed to be an entrance into the "real web site." They are basically used to trick the search engines for higher rankings.

o Also avoid signing up with SEO service companies that promise to get your web site in the top SERPs in one to two weeks. They typically use these tricky methods, and it will cost you in the long run. They may even get your site penalized by the search engines.

TACTICS YOU SHOULD USE:

- Remember to start a blog or forum for your web site if you have the time to do so. Although it does take time to maintain every couple of days, this is a great way to increase visits to your site and it increases your credibility even more. You can start a blog at www.blogger.com, or you can perform a Google search for other tools.

- You should also add new pages with interesting and relevant content every three to six months. Don't forget to include your keywords while keeping the keyword density at 1-2 percent. You should resubmit your web site to the search engines each time you add new content, change the meta tags, etc.

- Make sure to ask your customers and referrals how they found your web site. This information is vital in determining what methods bring you the most customers.

- You should monitor your rankings every few weeks. If your ranking has dropped more than a page behind, you should obtain more backlinks, add more content, and change keywords if necessary. You will not need to check rankings every day, because search engines don't change their results pages every day.

o It's not necessary to check your rankings for hundreds of keywords if you haven't optimized your web pages for those specific keywords.

- You should also stay informed on updates in the search engine optimization industry. I have included the following list of web sites that contain very helpful and up-to-date SEO info. Most of these web sites deliver e-mail newsletters that you can subscribe to:

  www.google.com/support/webmasters
  www.sitepronews.com
  www.webpronews.com
  http://searchengineland.com

I have suggested the web sites above since they provide the latest search engine information and deliver it right to your email on a regular basis. You won't even have to search for this helpful data.

- You will need to resubmit to the free directories when they have dropped your web site. The paid directories will require a renewal fee, depending on each directory.

- You should also grow your backlinks by submitting to additional directories every month or so. This will provide your web site with a solid link popularity.

- You should definitely run reports on your web site traffic on a regular basis. If your web hosting provider does not provide web statistics and metrics, you should consider changing to a different web host or purchasing software to keep track of all your site traffic. It is important to see which web page gets the most hits, how long visitors spend on your site, what search term led them to your site, etc. This way you know if your web site is performing well and receiving a good amount of traffic.

The following page contains a checklist of the major tactics you need to implement for top search engine rankings. You may want to make a copy of it to place by your computer.

SEO CHECKLIST TO HELP YOU STAY FOCUSED ON YOUR TASKS

Refer to the chapter listed with each checklist item for the guidelines you should follow while performing your search engine optimization:

✓ CHAPTER 2: Research your target market.

✓ CHAPTER 3: Perform a site audit.

✓ CHAPTER 4: Choose up to ten relevant keywords for your web site after performing keyword research.
> *Each page that has very different content should have different keywords to match content.

✓ CHAPTER 4–5: Provide substantial amounts of quality content with the proper keyword density of 1–2 percent and update it on a regular basis.

✓ CHAPTER 6: Submit one to two articles or press releases once a month for the first six to eight months.

✓ CHAPTER 6: Submit your web site to the major search engines after you make major changes to your web site information.

✓ CHAPTER 7: Keep analyzing your competitors' web sites and adjust your web site to keep up with the competition.

✓ CHAPTER 8: Create a robot.txt file and site map for your web site to make it easier for the search engine robots to access the pages on your site. Include alt tags for your images.

✓ CHAPTER 9: Obtain links from more directories and/or web sites. Try to attain as many links as your competitors. (NEVER BUY LINKS!)

✓ CHAPTER 10: Add different types of media, such as videos, images or blogs to your web site in the future.

✓ CHAPTER 11: Avoid the black hat SEO tactics discussed in this chapter and remember to implement the tactics recommended.

✓ EXTRA SUGGESTION: Stay updated with your market and trends and keep your web site updated with these trends.

IF YOU CHANGE THE TOPIC OF YOUR WEB SITE:

You or your web master need to change and insert the following code and/or files that you have previously included:

- Insert the meta tags with the new keywords, titles, and description.

- Insert your new keywords in the image alt tags.

- Change and upload the robot text file if you wish to exclude certain files in your web site from being accessed by the search engines.

- Change and upload the site map file if you need to update it when you add any new pages to your web site.

Keep your chin up during the entire process. It takes time and hard work to get top rankings, so remember this:

TO SUCCEED YOU MUST PERSEVERE. DON'T GIVE UP!

Glossary

Algorithm: an advanced formula with a set of rules used by search engines to evaluate a web site in determining its relevancy to a particular search. The search engines then rank the web sites within their indexes accordingly in their search results for a given query. Search engine companies keep the exact details of how algorithms work from the public.

Alt tag: an attribute included within an element link, most often an image link, to describe what the graphic is about; used to aid the vision impaired and search engine robots that cannot see images.

Anchor text: the text that contains a link embedded to another page of a web site.

Backlinks: all incoming links to a web page from an external web site; also referred to as inbound links.

Banned web pages: web pages extracted from a search engine's index and listings because of violating submission guidelines or performing spam.

Blog: an online, chronological publication of a person's comments/opinions on a given subject matter that are displayed as entries on a web page. Readers have the option to add their own entries to respond to the blogger's comments.

Crawler-based search engines: search engines that utilize a system of robots, or "crawlers," to scan entire web pages for information, and follow links on web sites to other web sites in order to register the information in their index. Most major search engines are crawler-based, including Google, Yahoo, MSN, and many others.

Domain: the online address of your web site, which is in the format: www.yourwebsite.com. It will direct the visitor to your web site when typed into any browser.

Doorway pages: html pages that are optimized with a large amount of keywords and are designed to be an entrance into the "real web site." This is an example of black hat SEO.

E-zine: an electronic version of a magazine or journal.

Flash: a program used to create animation or movies.

Forum: a web application that allows for discussion groups to be formed to discuss various topics. Participants can exchange open messages which are often monitored by moderators and are displayed in chronological order.

Google page rank: a method Google uses to assign a number between zero and ten to every web site on the Internet, also known as PR or Google PR.

HTML: an acronym for hypertext markup language; it is the fundamental coding language used to create web pages.

Index: the information a search engine contains, from which the search results are produced. It is basically made up of copies of web pages search engines have found from "crawling" the web.

Keyword: a word or phrase a web owner optimizes his/her web site for, in an effort to be highly listed in the search engines for the query on the keyword.

Keyword analysis: the method of researching the proper keywords a web owner desires their web site to rank highly for.

Keyword density: a ratio of the amount of times a keyword is used in relation to the total word count of the web page. It is calculated by dividing the times the keyword is mentioned by the total number of words on the page.

Link bait: online content that attracts other web site owners to link to it because of its unique value.

Link building: the system of building link popularity.

Link popularity: the measurement of how popular a page is based on the number of backlinks it has.

Link text: the text that is contained within a link and is visible to the reader. For example, <u>web hosting</u> is a link that contains the link text "web hosting."

Meta description tag: the meta tag that contains the description of the web page.

Meta keywords tag: the meta tag that contains the keywords of the web page.

Meta tags: data placed in the code of a web page that helps search engines decipher what the web page is about.

Organic listings: listings that search engines do not require payment for. Web sites appear based on their importance and relevance to the search query; also referred to as natural search results.

Organic search engine optimization: the method of developing and marketing a web site so that it achieves higher ranking in the search engine results pages (SERPs); also referred to as *organic SEO*.

Outbound links: links on a web page that lead the visitor to another external web site.

PPC: an acronym for pay-per-click.

Paid inclusion: an advertising program through which web owners can pay for their web site to be included in a search engine's index.

Paid placement: search engine listings available on search engines by payment only. They are guaranteed to be listed for the search query chosen by the advertiser.

Higher ranking can be achieved by paying more than other advertisers. Keywords are purchased through an auction, on a cost-per-click basis.

Query: the particular words or phrase a searcher types into a search engine form; also referred to as a search term.

ROI: an acronym for *return on investment*, representing the amount of profit produced from a particular project. It is calculated by subtracting the total amount of expenditures for the given project from the gross profit made, and then dividing by the expenditures.

$$ROI = \frac{(profit\ gained - cost\ of\ project)}{Cost\ of\ Project}$$

Rank/ranking: the position of a web site in the search results of a search engine for a given query.

Reciprocal link: when a web site contains a link to another web site in exchange for a backlink from the other web site.

Results pages: the listings of web sites that are displayed after a searcher enters a particular query; also referred to as SERPs, an acronym for *search engine results pages*.

Robots.txt: a simple text file of instruction code that alerts the search engine robots what to do with the information found on a web site.

SEM: an acronym for *search engine marketing*; also refers to a person or company that performs search engine marketing.

SEO: An acronym for *search engine optimization*; also refers to a person or company that performs search engine optimization.

SERPs: see results pages.

Search engine marketing: marketing a web site through search engines, which includes any of the following: organic search engine optimization (SEO), paid listings, etc.

Search terms: see query.

Social bookmarking: the method web visitors use to organize and share various web site links with others on social bookmarking sites including www.digg.com, www.furl.net, and www.blink.com.

Spam: in reference to search engines, spam includes any marketing method that has a negative impact on natural search results. Spamming methods include keyword stuffing, invisible text, and doorway pages; also referred to as black hat SEO.

Submission: to enter a web site URL for inclusion into a search engine's or directory's index. Acceptance is up to the search engine or directory.

INDEX